BHUTAN

Robert Cooper

MARSHALL CAVENDISH
New York • London • Sydney

CONTENTS

The Memorial Chorten is one of the most visible religious structures in the capital of Thimphu. It contains sacred religious paintings and tantric offerings.

CONTENTS

Traditional clothing is worn throughout Bhutan. Here, a Bhutanese girl is dressed in a *kira*. Its color, amount of decorative detail, and the quality of cloth reflect the social status of the person.

GEOGRAPHY

BHUTAN MEASURES ROUGHLY 93 miles (150 km) north to south and 186 miles (300 km) east to west. Apart from a southern strip that is barely 328 feet (100 m) above sea level, the country is mostly in the Himalayas, rising to an elevation of 24,792 feet (7,554 m) in the north.

The variations in climate are as extreme as the diversity in terrain. The southern strip is generally hot and humid, while the northern borders are under snow all year round. Regional climates can vary between valleys. The main rivers are usually deeply incised, and despite high rainfall throughout the country, agriculture is limited to areas close to perennial streams.

Centuries of isolation have protected Bhutan's forests and abundant flora and fauna, which like so much about Bhutan, are as they always were—untouched and beautiful.

Left: **Towering mountains and winding rivers sculpt the picturesque landscape of Bhutan.**

Opposite: **Bhutan has been described as a living museum because its ancient** *dzongs* **and temples remain the focus of modern life.**

PHYSICAL ENVIRONMENT

Like a giant staircase, Bhutan's topography rises steadily south-north from the semitropical low-lying flatlands of the southern Duars ("DOO-ars") to the valleys of the Central Himalayas at 3,282 to 9,846 feet (1,000 to 3,000 m), before giving way to the Great Himalaya Range, which towers well above 22,974 feet (7,000 m) along the Tibetan border.

Mountain chains averaging 9,800 feet (2,985 m) also run north-south from the Great Himalaya Range, physically isolating Bhutan's administrative regions in the western, central, and eastern parts of the country and greatly hindering attempts to improve interregional communications.

These physical divisions relate closely to ethnic divisions in Bhutan. They influence the type of crops people grow, their diet, the flora and fauna that surround them, the languages they speak, and even their politics.

Despite its small size, Bhutan is a land of great diversity, with dense jungles, valleys, alpine highlands, and towering snow peaks in close proximity to one another.

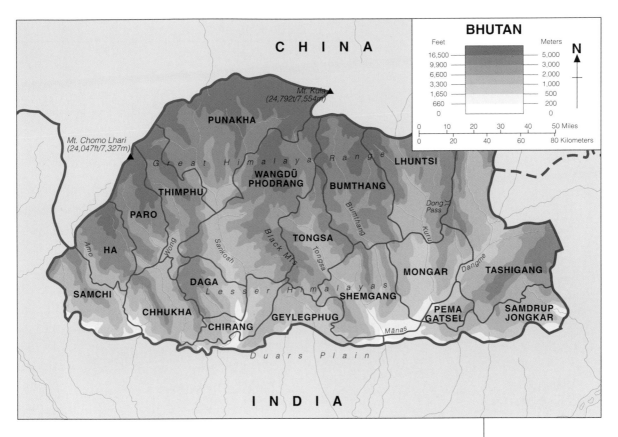

THE SOUTHERN DUARS

South of the Central Himalayan valleys and foothills lies the narrow Duars Plain, which forms a strip 8 to 10 miles (13 to 16 km) wide along the southern border of Bhutan. The Duars Plain is the wealthiest and most densely inhabited part of the country today.

The Duars area and the river valleys leading from it account for most of the fertile, cultivable land in the country. Where the land is not tilled by farmers, it quickly becomes tropical savannah and forest. In recent decades dams have been constructed to provide hydroelectricity, and large towns, more Indian in style than Bhutanese, have grown up along the border.

The 18 valleys of the Duars act as natural passages into a country that is composed almost entirely of mountains. This characteristic gave the region its name, which shares a derivation with the English word "doors."

The 16,738 feet (5,100 m) Yele La Pass. Bhutan is strategically located between China and India, controlling several key Himalayan mountain passes.

THE GREAT HIMALAYA RANGE

The northern part of Bhutan forms part of the Great Himalaya Range, which radiates south into the Central Himalayas. The snow-capped Himalayan range reaches heights of over 24,615 feet (7,500 m) and extends along the Bhutan-China border.

Historically, communication with Tibet in the north has been more important than with India in the south. Although the Great Himalaya Range divides Bhutan and Tibet and covers 20% of Bhutan in perpetual snow, there are four *la* ("LAH") or mountain passes linking the two countries. These *la* follow the course of rivers that over millennia have cut their way deeply into the rock and earth, crossing into Bhutan at altitudes significantly lower than the mountain peaks. As a result, at certain times of the year, it was easier and safer to travel to Tibet than to India.

The jagged peaks support no life except, perhaps, that of the gods, as the Bhutanese believe. The people treat the Himalayas with great respect, and some peaks are considered sacred. Since passage to Tibet is always through mountain passes, some of which remain open all winter, the Bhutanese have no reason to climb the peaks.

The Kholong River bisects the mountainous territory and flows south into the Brahmaputra River in India.

RIVERS

Rivers are an important source of electricity and revenue for Bhutan. Due to high precipitation and a wide variation in altitude, Bhutan has a huge potential for hydroelectric power. However, only a few dams have been built to date. Since domestic requirements are modest, the majority of the energy produced is exported to India.

There are four main river systems running from west to east in Bhutan—the Manas, the Sankosh, the Wong, and the Amo. All originate in the Himalayas, with several entering Bhutan from Tibet.

The Manas, which follows a circuitous route in the west of the country, is often cited as Bhutan's biggest river because it contain the greatest amount of water.

Bhutan's rivers have many rapids and waterfalls. The country also receives a tremendous amount of rain every year. As a result, none of the rivers are navigable. They carry vital nutrients from the glacial Himalayas and deposit them in the fertile lands of the upper-central valleys and the southern lowlands before passing through the Duars region and crossing into India, where they eventually join the Brahmaputra River.

CLIMATE

Primarily because of variations in altitude, Bhutan's climate differs greatly among regions, more so than any other similar-sized area in the world. Three principal climatic regions can be identified—humid and subtropical in the southern plains, temperate climate with cool winters and hot summers in the central valleys, and severe winters and cool summers in the Himalayas. April and May are mostly windy with occasional showers. Strong gusts of wind arrive most afternoons, raising clouds of dust and threatening the roofs of simpler houses.

Like most of Asia, Bhutan experiences the monsoons. The summer monsoon, which lasts from June to September, brings heavy rain from the southwest. As the monsoon sets in, days can pass with hardly a letup in the downpour. However, a rhythm soon develops, with most of the rain falling in the evenings and at night.

In the highest mountain regions, rivers are permanently frozen into glaciers.

THE BLUE POPPY

The blue poppy was once thought to be a myth like the Yeti—its existence was much talked about but not verified. Confirmed only in 1933 by a British botanist in Bhutan, it remains extremely rare, growing only above the tree line at an elevation of around 13,128 feet (4,000 m). Known in the national language of Bhutan as *euitgel metog hoem* ("AYT-gel meyt-og hoaym"), the blue poppy has a life span of three to five years. It grows up to 3 feet (1 m) tall, flowers once at the beginning of the rains, then produces seed and dies.

FLORA

The dramatic changes in altitude and climate in this small country have resulted in a rich array of flora. Moreover, most of Bhutan's flora remain undisturbed so Bhutan probably has the richest flora in the Himalayan region. Within a distance of 62 miles (100 km), the rice paddies and fruit orchards of the south give way successively to deciduous forests and alpine forests, arriving finally at grassy meadows and fields of barley and winter wheat set among the mountains.

Bhutan has been called a botanical paradise. There are more than 5,000 known plant species including the edelweiss, the blue poppy (Bhutan's national flower), carnivorous plants, almost every type of orchid, giant rhubarb, and magnolia.

Over 300 species of locally-grown medicinal plants can be found in Bhutan, which has been called the Land of Medicinal Plants. The building of roads, started in the 1960s, carried a threat to Bhutan's soft and hardwood forests. Fortunately the king has led the government in a major effort to protect the environment.

FORESTS

At altitudes below 3,000 feet (914 m)—all in the south and the Duars valleys extending into Bhutan—the forests are tropical. The most valuable forests in Bhutan are located between 3,282 to 9,846 feet (1,000 to 3,000 m), where cypress, fir, spruce, and juniper can be found.

Until the beginning of the 20th century, the tropical forests formed a dangerous barrier to the south containing two feared creatures—the tiger and the malarial mosquito. To the Bhutanese, who were used to higher, cooler climates where mosquitoes cannot survive, the lowlands were a menace of disease that had to be crossed to get to their southern neighbors.

The Bhutanese were uninterested in exploiting the forest resources and were happy to lease off large tracts in the south to Assam. Forest cover gradually shrank back from the western borders as Nepali immigrants arrived throughout the first half of the 20th century, cut the forests, planted rice and orchard crops, and built the existing small border towns.

Bhutanese, who had little use for the land, welcomed the immigrants and encouraged migration by providing free land deeds and economic assistance. The inevitable result was that Bhutan had more people, more marketable produce, but fewer trees.

Until roads were built to the south in the 1960s, everybody was happy with the situation. Bhutanese had no way of transporting their forest produce and therefore did not seek control of the forests until well into the 20th century.

In 1986 the Royal Society for the Protection of Nature was established to raise national awareness of Bhutan's natural treasures, and in 1991 a trust fund was set up with money provided from the World Wildlife Fund and several European governments to assist Bhutan's conservation efforts.

The system of national parks was rapidly expanded, protected forest areas were increased, and forestry education was greatly extended.

It is still too early to evaluate the success of conservation programs which face two major hurdles. The first, the traditional method of farming, especially in the east, involves cutting down trees, setting them on fire and planting in the ashes. The other hurdle is the reliance of most Bhutanese on firewood as cooking and heating fuel.

To solve these problems, efforts have begun to supply alternative fuels, at least in the urban areas, and to teach responsible and efficient harvesting of firewood. Education and fertilizer are said to be the twin tools for changing traditional farming methods into more forest-friendly systems. A harder line has been taken against tree poaching, and the transportation of trees and forest products into India is now closely controlled.

Commercial logging is controlled, and oak, pine, and tropical hardwoods are the main species harvested.

Yaks, a common form of livestock in Bhutan, are concentrated in the west of the country.

FAUNA

In Bhutan the fauna is as varied as the flora. The World Wildlife Fund records 165 species of mammals, including many rare animals such as the golden langur, snow leopard, and red panda. Like the flora and the human population, different species of animal tend to prefer different habitats.

The southern forests are home to elephants, tigers, rhinoceros, wild buffalos, many snakes, and several species of monkey, including the golden langur, a small primate discovered only in the 20th century and believed to live only in southern Bhutan.

The central Himalayas host black bears, red pandas, hornbills, wild boar, and the famous black-necked cranes, a rarity among the 625 species of birds recorded in Bhutan.

Northern areas above the tree line and the high valleys are the habitats of yaks, blue sheep, mountain goats, and Bhutan's national animal, the takin, a migratory pasturalist said to have a cow's body and a sheep's head. This is also the home of the extremely rare snow leopard, whose beautiful coat has resulted in over-hunting and strict conservation measures.

THE BLACK-NECKED CRANES

These endangered birds migrate from Siberia and Tibet in mid-October to specific valleys in Bhutan, leaving again when spring arrives. They are very much a part of the local folklore, and Bhutanese who live in those areas hosting the 300 to 400 birds believe that they bring good luck. The Royal Society for the Protection of Nature has introduced a Black-Necked Crane Festival, first held in November 1998. It was so popular with Bhutanese and foreigners that it is now an annual event.

CITIES

More than 90% of Bhutanese live in small, scattered villages and rely on agriculture and livestock for their livelihood. They come to town for free medical services, to go to market, and increasingly to get an education, but few aspire to live in the kind of urban sprawl that exists on the other side of the southern frontier.

Urban settlements did not exist until the 1960s. They followed the construction of roads and economic development. Bhutan's capital, Thimphu, lies in a beautiful, wooded valley and is the largest urban area in Bhutan. There is only one main road, and while some of the new buildings are less than inspiring, traditional architecture predominates.

Thimphu is one of the least populated capitals in the world with a population of 40,000.

HISTORY

BHUTAN'S HISTORY IS A RECIPE that combines folklore, British explorers, Tibetan monks and soldiers, and the rare manuscripts that have survived the feuds of warlords, earthquakes, and fires.

Mystery shrouds Bhutan's distant past. Its history is ambiguous, and for most Bhutanese, incomprehensible without reference to at least some mythology, which the average Bhutanese considers to be as real as history verified by material evidence.

The strong belief in reincarnation means that important persons may be known by several names. The times they lived in are not always clearly distinguished.

Similarly, the belief in Tantric Buddhism is so deeply ingrained that a history of Bhutan would make no sense without inclusion of the main religious teachers.

Left: The wheel of reincarnation. Buddhists believe that all life forms experience an endless cycle of rebirths, and only through enlightenment can they be released from this cycle.

Opposite: Throughout Bhutan, prayer flags of blue, green, red, yellow, and white are mounted on long poles and placed at holy as well as dangerous locations. Bhutanese believe that the flags ward off demons and help to build merit.

Nomadic herders in Bhutan. Their lifestyle is not very much different from that of their ancestors' 4,000 years ago.

EARLY HISTORY

Bhutan has yet to undertake any real archaeological research. Therefore any discovery could radically change the picture we have of the region's pre- and ancient history.

Man-made stone implements found on the surface and dating as early as 2,000 B.C. suggest the first inhabitants were nomadic herders who spent the summer on the natural pasturage of the higher elevations, where it was unnecessary to cut down trees; in winter they lived in the more sheltered valleys, where firewood and forest foods were plentiful.

Other than that, little is known about the first inhabitants. It is presumed that they had an animistic religion, which typically predated Buddhism in other parts of the Himalayas, but any further conjecture on lifestyle and beliefs must await the future findings of archaeologists.

BUDDHISM

The written history of Bhutan began with Buddhist literature and chronicles. Buddhism arrived in Bhutan in the 7th century, when Tibetan king, Srongtsen Gampo, ordered the construction of the first two Buddhist temples—one at Kyichu in the Paro Valley and the other at Bumthang in central Bhutan. Both temples remain today and are popular with pilgrims.

In the eighth century a Buddhist teacher known as Padmasambhava or Guru Rimpoche (Precious Master) brought the essence of Tantric Buddhism to Bhutan and Tibet and established the Nyingmapa school of thought. All Bhutanese also regard him as the Second Buddha because of the miraculous powers he was said to possess. The many places in which Guru Rimpoche meditated are destinations of pilgrimage and worship for most Bhutanese.

Perched on a cliff overlooking the Paro Valley, the Taktsang Monastery is Bhutan's most photographed site. It is said that Guru Rimpoche flew there on the back of a tiger in the eighth century.

The assassination of a Tibetan king in A.D. 842 threw Tibet into turmoil for two centuries. During this time, Tibetan aristocrats fled Tibet with their followers and settled in the central and eastern valleys of Bhutan. They brought with them the origins of the conflicts in Tibet, so until the 16th century, Bhutan suffered an intermittent civil war in which almost every valley fought against its neighbors, and none of the contending warlords could gain the upper hand.

Against this tumultuous background in the 16th century, religious thought developed and segmented in Bhutan. Innovation again entered from Tibet, this time by Phajo Drugom Shigpo, who waged a successful struggle against the Lhapas of western Bhutan, built monasteries at Phajoding and Tango. Phajo Drugom Shigpo taught the Bhutanese interpretations of the Drukpa ("DROOK-pah"). *Druk* means thunder dragon, and *pa* refers to a sect and the people belonging to that particular sect. Thus the name Drukpa came to Bhutan.

Today the inhabitants who reside in the western part of Bhutan, and by extension the citizens of the entire country, are known as Drukpa, which means "people of the thunder dragon."

UNIFICATION

For the first time in its history, Bhutan became politically unified in the 17th century under Ngawang Namgyal, another religious leader from Tibet. Ngawang Namgyal (1594–1651) belonged to the Drukpa school and brought with him the title of Shabdrung, which translates as "at whose feet one prostrates." His authority in Tibet had been based on recognition that he was the reincarnation of a famous Drukpa scholar, Pema Karpo (1527–92). After a series of victories over rival subsect leaders, Ngawang Namgyal became the first leader to unite Bhutan under one rule.

During his leadership, Ngawang Namgyal developed a dual system of government that distinguishes a spiritual leader from a secular (government) leader. He also introduced the system of *dzongs* in Bhutan, the first of which was constructed at Simtokha in the Wong River Valley. The *dzong* served as an impregnable fortress where the population could retreat in case of an attack. In addition, it housed a monastery and administrative offices. The same model of combined defense, religion, and administration was replicated in all subsequent *dzongs*.

Opposite: **A religious icon of Guru Rimpoche. He is the father of the Tantric Buddhism practiced in Bhutan.**

DRUKPA KUNLEY

One of the most popular figures in Bhutanese history was Drukpa Kunley (1455–1529). Known as "the divine madman" because of his shocking behavior, Drukpa Kunley was an eccentric person. An aristocrat from the great Gya family, he refused to take his monastic vows and instead wandered the country teaching Buddhism through songs. It is difficult to attribute historical significance to Drukpa Kunley, although every Bhutanese will place him among the most important national historical characters.

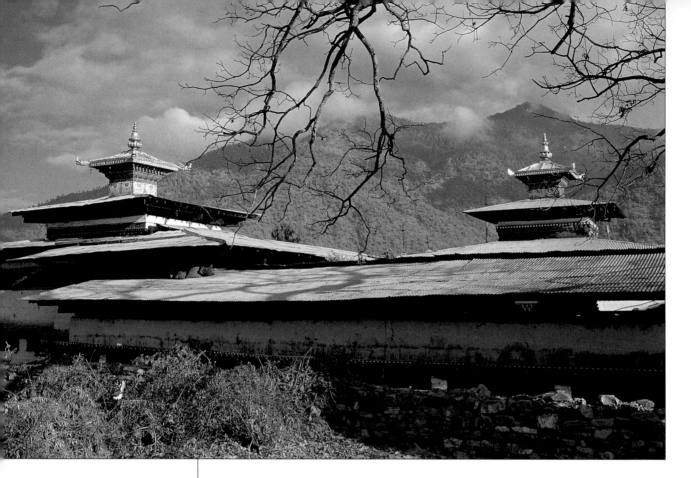

The Kyichu Lhakhang Dzong is located in Paro, which houses the largest, oldest, and most spectacular *dzongs* in the kingdom.

Freed from the constant need for military defence, Shabdrung Ngawang Namgyal consolidated the political and religious power of the Drukpas in western Bhutan. He turned his attention to diplomacy, winning rights to establish and control monasteries in Tibet and Nepal, where Bhutanese monasteries were to become among the most famous of Nepal's tourist sights at Boudanath and Swayanbunath, and where Bhutanese remained in charge until the Nepal-Tibet wars of 1854–56. The Shabdrung did not live to see the full unification of central and eastern Bhutan, which was formally accomplished in 1656, five years after his death in 1651.

With this unification, Bhutan took on its definitive shape, but the country as a whole lacked a name. It was called variously *Loh Jong* (Southern Valleys), *Loh Mon Kha Shi* (Southern Mon Country of Four Approaches), *Loh Jong Men Jong* (Southern Valleys of Medicinal Plants), and *Loh Mon Tsenden Jong* (Southern Mon Valleys Where Sandalwood and Cypress Grow). The Drukpas then decided to name the country after themselves—Druk Yul, Land of the Thunder Dragon.

BEYOND THE GRAVE

During his rule, Shabdrung Ngawang Namgyal gave Bhutan its system of administration and law. Buddhist moral principles and customary law of that time were welded into a national legal system, and laws were administered by a theocracy of monks, presided over by the *je khenpo* (chief abbot) and a secular chief or *desi*. The dual system of spiritual and temporal power was unified and transcended by the person who assumed the title of the Shabdrung, whose authority was at once that of the order of monks and the force of secular law.

The manner of the Shabdrung's leaving the world was as remarkable as his reign, and in a sense he ruled from beyond the grave for over 50 years.

In 1651 the Shabdrung went into retreat at Punakha Dzong. Lengthy retreats are common in Tantric Buddhism, where monks can spend years without any outside communication. Thus, his failure to appear could be expected to attract little attention in a land where news took weeks to travel from one side of the small country to the other.

It is believed the Shabdrung died in 1651. News of his death was concealed from the people by the *desis* and *je khenpos* until 1705—an incredible period of 54 years, during which the people went on believing the Shabdrung was meditating on their behalf. During this time, Tibet attacked repeatedly and was beaten back every time. Folklore says that the Shabdrung gave the orders for the defense of Drukyul.

The Shabdrung system of power control required a strong man at the top. Unfortunately, internal conflict emerged in the early part of the 18th century, and power struggles within and between the *dzongs* greatly weakened the Shabdrung's system of government. It was in a weakened state that Druk Yul was to encounter the might of the British.

THE BRITISH

The British East India Company initially had little interest in Bhutan until it expanded into the Kingdom of Cooch Bazaar on Bhutan's southern border in 1772; the Honorable Company, as it called itself, was more interested in Cooch Bazaar, and a request from the dethroned king of Cooch Bazaar for Company's intervention resulted in a 1772 military action which routed the Bhutanese and restored the King of Cooch Bazaar.

British officers and Indian troops chased the Bhutanese into Bhutan and beat them in battles at Wong River, near Phuntsholing, and at Kalimpong, now in India on Bhutan's western flank. The results of this impressive British show of strength made an impact on Bhutan. Failing to receive help from Tibet, the new *desi* was eager to make an agreement with the Company. In 1774 both parties signed a treaty in which the *desi* of Bhutan agreed to respect the territories of the East India Company and to allow the Company to cut timber in Bhutan's forests. In return, Bhutan received back all territory captured by the British.

The British

Relations between the two countries remained friendly until 1826, when the British took control of Assam, which borders much of Bhutan's south. Very soon, control and occupation of the Duars area, which had been under Assamese control through a complex agreement with Bhutan, was cause for conflict between the Company and Bhutan's rulers.

Relations deteriorated until the British annexed the Bhutanese-controlled Assam Duars in 1841 in exchange for an annual compensation payment. The Company's plans to clear the malarial forests and plant tea on Bhutan's slopes were shelved following British involvement in the Afghan War, the Anglo-Sikh War, and finally the Indian Mutiny in 1857.

The Bhutanese took advantage of Britain's preoccupations to raid the Company-controlled Duars and Cooch Bazaar, capturing elephants and kidnapping British subjects. The British were furious. Relations went downhill so badly that in November 1864 British forces occupied the remaining Duars area, gaining control of the whole of southern Bhutan.

A Bhutanese counterattack in January 1865 was successful in driving British troops out of Bhutan but not for long. Fierce fighting continued until Bhutan had no choice but to sign away control of the Duars area in perpetuity to the British and to guarantee Britain's trade interests in return for an annuity of 50,000 rupees.

With India's independence from Britain, Bhutan was recognized as an independent state. The two countries signed a treaty in 1949, in which most of the territory taken by Britain, including the Duars region, was returned (except for Kalimpong) and Bhutan agreed to be guided in its foreign affairs by India.

By that time the Shabdrung theocracy had been replaced by a formalized division of religious and secular powers, with the secular realm under the control of a hereditary monarchy, the Wangchuck dynasty, which rules Bhutan today.

A year after Bhutan received the 50,000 rupees, the country was ceded to the East India Company.

GOVERNMENT

THE INTERNAL CONFLICTS OF BHUTAN CONTINUED UNTIL 1885, when Ugyen Wangchuck defeated his political enemies and brought Bhutan under one rule. At that time, British power was dominant throughout the subcontinent, and Ugyen Wangchuck favored increased cooperation with the British. In 1904 Ugyen accompanied the British invasion of Tibet and assisted in a negotiated settlement between Tibet and Britain. In recognition of his services and status, he received the British title of Knight Commander of the Indian Empire.

Following three decades of peace under the rule of Ugyen, the secular and religious leaders came together and unanimously elected him King of Bhutan. On December 17, 1907, Ugyen Wangchuck was crowned with the title Druk Gyalpo (Dragon King), and Bhutan's system of hereditary monarchy began with the Wangchuck dynasty.

Left: **The Trashichhoe Dzong was renovated in the 1960s and now houses the offices of the king and the central body governing the monks.**

Opposite: **A military parade celebrates a festival in Bhutan.**

GLORIOUS ISOLATION

Good relations with Britain and its neighbors on the subcontinent did not change Bhutan's policy of isolation.

The second king of Bhutan, King Jigme Wangchuck, succeeded his father Ugyen Wangchuck and ruled from 1926 to 1952, a tumultuous time that saw World War, the Great Depression, and violent independence movements.

The outside world had little to offer Bhutan, and Bhutan, having never been colonized, had little need to open its doors. King Jigme therefore concentrated his efforts on strengthening the internal administrative and taxation systems, as well as centralizing control over a country that remained geographically fractured into valleys and *dzongs*. Bhutan's continued isolation was blessed with decades of peace at home, in contrast to the conflicts beyond its borders.

However, this isolation was not absolute. King Wangchuck sent his son and heir to India and England to be educated. Financial aid from Britain enabled the construction of the first Western-style schools in Bhutan and was also used to send the first Bhutanese students for advanced education in India.

MODERNIZATION

When the third king, Jigme Dorji Wangchuck, succeeded his father in 1952, he wasted no time in leading Bhutan gently toward modernization. He abolished slavery and serfdom in 1956 and invited the Indian prime minister Jawaharjal Nehru for an official visit in 1958. With China taking control of Tibet on Bhutan's northern border, it became obvious to the king that isolationism was no longer the best survival tactic.

In 1961 the king launched Bhutan's first five-year plan with an emphasis on road building and the construction of the huge Chhukha River hydroelectric project. In 1962 Bhutan joined the Colombo Plan and gained access to technical assistance and training facilities. In 1966 the king moved the capital to Thimphu to increase the efficiency of government administration. In 1971 Bhutan joined the United Nations. It also established formal diplomatic relations with another country for the first time, by allowing an Indian ambassador to reside in Bhutan and sending an ambassador to India to represent Bhutan.

Above: **Traditional architecture predominates in modern Thimphu. Pictured is a gasoline station.**

Opposite: **The majority of the population live in small, scattered villages, although urban settlements have sprung up since the late 1960s.**

The king's achievements were impressive. Dzongkha was made the national language during his rule. He also set up Bhutan's Tshogdu (National Assembly) and drew up a 12-volume written code of law. He redistributed land to the poor, created the Royal Bhutan Army, introduced a national police force, and established the High Court.

In addition, he carried out other development projects, which included the establishment of a national museum in Paro, a national library, national archives, and a national stadium. Due to his progressive initiatives, King Jigme Dorji Wangchuck is regarded as the "Father of Modern Bhutan." The present monarch King Jigme Singye Wangchuck has continued the policy of controlled development.

The building housing the National Museum in Paro was built in 1656.

HIS MAJESTY KING JIGME SINGYE WANGCHUCK

King Jigme Dorji Wangchuck died in 1972 at the age of 44. His son, Jigme Singye Wangchuck, ascended the throne on June 2, 1974 at the age of 17 (Picture shows the king then).

Bhutan's era of isolation ended at his coronation, an occasion witnessed for the first time by the international press. The king is credited as the architect of modern education, the creator of Bhutan's free national health service, a builder of roads, an initiator of conservation programs, a reformer, and a diplomat. Under his leadership, Bhutan has joined most UN agencies, the Movement of Nonaligned Countries, and the South Asian Association for Regional Cooperation. He has broadened diplomatic representation to 21 countries, including Bangladesh, India, Japan, Switzerland, and the European Community. Gradually, he has lifted restrictions on foreigners visiting Bhutan. In an effort to modernize Bhutan's political system and reduce the power of the monarch, King Wangchuck introduced a package of democratic reforms that granted power to the legislature, through a vote of no confidence, to depose the king in favor of his successor.

While a tremendous amount has been accomplished in a short period, the king has been consciously aware of the need to preserve the environment and retain the special character of Bhutan's people, while promoting national identity built on traditional values. He lists his development goals as self-reliance, sustainability, efficiency and development of the private sector, people's participation and decentralization, human resource development, and last of all, regionally balanced development. While economic self-reliance is Bhutan's goal, commercial interests must be in harmony with the policy of environmental conservation and must work for the greater benefit of "One Nation, One People." The king himself has summed up his policy goals in the phrase "gross national happiness."

The world's youngest reigning monarch is married to four sisters.

THE CENTRAL GOVERNMENT

The king is the head of state. He is also the head of government, assisted by a cabinet consisting of ministers and representatives from the full range of ministries and special commissions, and the chief of the army and police. Each ministry is divided into departments, each headed by a director.

NATIONAL ASSEMBLY

The main functions of the Tshogdu or National Assembly are to enact laws, approve senior appointments in the government, and advise on all matters of national importance. It normally meets as a body twice a year and currently consists of 154 members, made up of 105 *chimis* ("CHI-mi"), elected by the people as representatives of Bhutan's 20 districts for three-year terms; 37 nominated senior civil servants, including 20 *dzongdas* ("DZONG-dar") or district officers, who change according to appointment; and another 12 representatives of religious orders, who serve for three years.

The Tshogdu elects from among its members a speaker, who may convene special sessions on urgent matters. Any Bhutanese over the age of 25 can run for election to the Tshogdu. A secret ballot may be called for, but most decisions are passed by simple majority. A unique characteristic of the Tshogdu is that it has the power to replace the monarch by a two-thirds vote and may also take a vote of no confidence in the king.

LEGISLATURE

The Tshogdu is the national legislative body. Unlike in other monarchies, decisions of the assembly do not require royal assent. The king has no power of veto over any resolution or statute of the Tshogdu. The code of civil and criminal law is a modification of that set down by Shabdrung Ngawang Namgyal in the 17th century.

Below: **King Jigme Dorji Wangchuck took the initiative to adapt Bhutan's system of government to the modern era and in 1953 established the Tshogdu.**

Opposite: **The present King of Bhutan, His Majesty Jigme Singye Wangchuck and one of his four queens.**

ECONOMY

DEVELPMENT PROJECTS AND MODERNIZATION of the health services, education, telecommunications, postal service, roads, and public transport have greatly increased the Bhutanese' with the outside world in recent decades.

Despite these developments, the daily life of most Bhutanese has changed little since the 17th century. About 85 to 90% of the population is still dependent on farming for a livelihood. They use the same tools as their forefathers, grow the same subsistence crops, use oxen to pull their ploughs, and come together in kinship and neighbor groups to share labor-intensive activities. Such farmers might listen to a radio and hear the news from India, but they are more likely to aspire to own a horse than an automobile. Apart from public services and small-scale enterprises, employment in the modern sectors of the economy is limited.

Left: **A post office in Bumthang, the spiritual heartland of Bhutan.**

Opposite: **A small grocery store in Paro caters to the daily needs of the local population.**

SOURCES OF REVENUE

Agriculture and livestock-raising are still regarded as the main pillars of the economy because the great majority of people could not survive without them. However, these activities contribute only about 40% of the gross national product. The biggest single export is electricity, which provides 25% of the total revenue. Forestry and forest products account for some 15%, while industry and mining together account for 10%. Tourism, which has expanded many times since the 1960s, also earns important foreign exchange. One of Bhutan's more unusual sources of revenue, considering that the postal service was introduced only recently, is postage stamps.

The Bhutanese monetary system is based on the ngultrum, which was established in 1974.

AGRICULTURE AND LIVESTOCK

Only 7.8% of the land is under cultivation, and most of that is in the south. Cash crops account for one-quarter of the country's export earnings, and the rest is for subsistence living. Agricultural specialties include tangerine oranges, which are sold widely on the subcontinent, cardamom, and temperate fruits. Potatoes, corn, rice, millet, wheat, buckwheat, barley, mustard, and vegetables are also exported.

Above the subtropical line, where access to a cash market is problematic, priority is placed on growing subsistence cereal crops to feed the family. All farmers keep livestock to produce milk products and provide draught power. At higher altitudes, little cultivation is possible, but there are wide areas of natural grasslands that provide pasture for cattle, sheep, and yaks.

The emphasis on self-sufficiency has ensured that most Bhutanese have their own family plots where they can grow enough to feed the family. Anyone who feels he does not have enough land can petition the king for more; such petitions are frequently granted.

In Bhutan, women are every bit as involved in agricultural activities as men.

Bhutan's fast-flowing rivers provide abundant potential hydroelectricity and help to support capital-intensive industries such as forestry and mining.

HYDROELECTRICITY

It has been estimated that Bhutan has the potential to generate 30,000 megawatts of hydroelectric power. Currently, the Chukha project generates a tiny fraction of that potential, producing 336 megawatts, of which 78% is exported. Other projects include the Tala, also on the Wong River, which is set to produce over 1,000 megawatts, much of which will be exported to India. There are smaller projects of 60 megawatts near Mongar and Wangdü Phodrang. Given Bhutan's potential and the energy needs of an industrializing India, the government's plan to fund Bhutan's entire national budget from revenues obtained from the sale of hydroelectricity appears realistic.

Bhutan's hydroelectric projects are consistent with the national philosophy of development, as they harness the power of Bhutan's rivers without building large dams. As such, the hydroelectric projects do not require the sacrifice of large areas of productive farmland, are clean, and may be considered environmentally friendly.

POWER TO THE PEOPLE

Hydroelectric projects exist in areas where they can produce the greatest benefit for the smallest input of funds and labor, and where they are near to the buyer. To construct transmission lines to serve all of Bhutan's scattered population, however, would be unsightly and expensive. Thus, many Bhutanese have yet to experience the benefits of electricity at home. Instead, a proportion of the income from the sale of energy is used to develop micro-hydroelectric facilities throughout the country. Where hydroelectricity is not feasible in the remote regions, it is replaced by solar power. Through these means, the government plans to introduce electricity to all schools, monasteries, and eventually to all homes.

Although rivers provide low-cost energy, some remote villages and farmhouses have yet to experience the benefits of electricity.

Forests are one of Bhutan's most significant natural resources, and the country has so far been able to balance revenue needs and ecological considerations.

FORESTRY

Bhutan's development philosophy of encouraging sustainability is most evident in its forestry industry. With about 60% of the country covered in forest and new roads facilitating exploitation, the temptation to follow the lead of other developing countries and sell off the forests to gain sufficient foreign capital to jump-start the economy must have been strong.

Such a temptation has been resisted in Bhutan, and in practice, quite the opposite has taken place. Bhutan has reduced the amount of timber and forest product it sells to India and places guards and road blocks in place to limit log poaching. The forestry industry is controlled, and any expansion will take place only after detailed consideration.

These actions stem from the values that constrain Bhutanese from taking the next generation's resources ("permanent treasures") for the gain of the current generation ("temporary pleasures"). In light of this, the relative importance of forestry as an export earner is not likely to rise above the current 15% of the gross national product.

EXPORT INDUSTRIES

Bhutan is one of the least industrialized countries in the world and it is not complaining. There is no indication that an industrial revolution will ever arrive in Bhutan, and if it did, it would certainly be resisted by the government. This is not to say that Bhutanese have turned their backs on the benefits of modernization. They simply prefer to keep what they have before trying anything new. In addition, anything new must conform to the values of society, and be environmentally friendly and economically sound resource use, while maintaining resource sustainability. On a global scale, that is a tall order.

Bhutan seems set to succeed because it has a small population, compared to its resources, as well as an abundance of potential clean and sustainable energy. The majority of its population who are Buddhists, also hold a positive attitude. They see conservation and sustainability as intrinsically good. The priority is always to maintain subsistence production and feed the family; therefore production on top of basic needs must not take people away from their land at significant times. Given this background, it is perhaps surprising that Bhutan has managed to build an export industry through what appears to be an all-gain-and-no-pain process.

Furniture of good quality is exported to India. Matsutake mushrooms are cultivated in the west of the country and exported to Japan, Singapore, and Thailand. Bhutan's temperate fruits find markets in neighboring countries and serve as the base for a growing industry of canning fruit and

Cottage industries, where the people make and sell small produce at home, are common in rural settlements.

43

making jam, which, along with various types of alcoholic spirits, are marketed cheaply under the Druk label to India, Nepal, and more distant neighbors. A cement factory exports large quantities of cement to India and Bangladesh.

One successful new enterprise fully in line with the national philosophy is the production of oil from lemongrass. The villagers use comparatively simple equipment to distil the oil from fast-growing weed, which needs to be cut down anyway. The product is small and easily transportable, making it an ideal enterprise for the remote eastern villages where the industry has grown up. The oil is sold to Germany where it goes into perfumes and deodorants, and profits return directly to villagers, who use the money to improve their farming methods and purchase some of the benefits of the modern world. So successful has the project been that the villages are now diversifying into pine oil and oil of other plants that thrive in Bhutan, such as rhododendron and juniper.

An unusual export is postage stamps. Remarkable in both form and content, these stamps are deliberately produced by the post office with an eye on foreign collectors. They come in various forms, including stamps made of metal and silk, three-dimensional images, and mini-phonograph records. Printed on them are pictures of Bhutanese *dzongs*, flowers, animals, mountains, people, and even Mickey Mouse and other Disney characters.

PUTTING SILKWORMS ABOVE DEVELOPMENT

One development project rejected by Bhutan was the expansion of its domestic silk industry. This would have required throwing silkworm cocoons alive into boiling water to ensure long threads of silk. Bhutanese allow the silkworms to eat their way out of their silk cocoons, thus spoiling the thread but allowing the silkworms to fulfill their destiny.

TOURISM

The coronation of the present monarch His Majesty Jigme Singye Wangchuck on June 2, 1974 was witnessed by the international media and many foreigners, marking Bhutan's appearance on the world stage. Previously any foreign visitors to Bhutan had come as guests of the king or other members of the royal family. The visitors who attended the ceremony were welcomed as guests, and accommodation was specially constructed for them. When they left, this accommodation was available to the first small groups of tourists.

Aware that there were many young Western travelers waiting for the chance to enter the seemingly forbidden country of Bhutan, the government initially limited the number of tourists to 200 each year, and costs were set at US$130 per day. Tourists were also restricted to Phuntsholing, Paro, and Thimphu. They had a difficult time getting to Bhutan, which had no airport and required entry through Phuntsholing, which in turn required a permit from India, which took six weeks to arrange.

Visitors to Bhutan pay a daily tariff of US$200, a price which includes accomodation.

45

Druk Air, Bhutan's national airline, operates between Paro and India, Nepal, Bangladesh, and Thailand.

Very gradually the quota of tourists increased, and the itinerary was expanded. By the time Bhutan's airport opened at Paro in 1983, the national airline, Druk Air, delivered tourists directly from Calcutta or Kathmandu, avoiding ground transit through India.

In 1991 private travel agents were allowed to operate, with rules and charging rates laid down by the Tourism Association of Bhutan. Tourists were allowed more varied itineraries, which covered a greater part of the inner Himalayas, but for their own safety they were restricted from visiting the south, troubled in the late 1980s and 1990s by political disturbances.

As in all other ventures with the outside world, Bhutan has embarked on tourism with caution. The Bhutanese are determined to preserve their unique culture, and therefore when in doubt, they stop, set rules and regulations, and monitor well before making any change. This development philosophy has kept the character of the country intact and made Bhutan an even more attractive tourist experience.

TRANSPORTATION

Before the 1960s, transportation—even for royalty visiting abroad—meant travel by foot and muleback, days between destinations, and primitive facilities all the way. The first roads that were built in the early 1960s followed the old north-south lines of Bhutan's Duars, connecting Thimphu and other towns in the central axis of the country with the Indian border to the south. By this means, centers of population and administration were physically connected to India, but not to each other.

The isolated valleys, which had been so formative in Bhutan's history are separated by high, north-south ridges, with few connecting passes. Although some curvy roads exist now, east-west travel for most of the population continues to involve a lot of time and legwork.

Perhaps the greatest benefit of Bhutan's new roads is the opening up to international markets. However, this has tended to increase imports from India and from elsewhere via India, rather than to increase exports. Trucks and buses ply the new routes, and along with the goods of the

Prior to the construction of roads in the 1960s, travel in Bhutan was by foot or on muleback or horseback.

modern world, they carry people and new ideas. India and Bhutan have an agreement that allows citizens of either country to travel and work freely in the other. While change has been controlled, the road blocks set up to stop the illegal export of timber do not slow the introduction of new ideas.

Bhutan was one of the last countries in the world to develop facilities for air travel. The opening of Paro airport in 1983 marked an important step in Bhutan's dialogue with the world. To the businessperson, particularly from India, visiting Thimphu to discuss business today is no more difficult than going to any city in India.

In Bhutan buses are operated by government-owned as well as private companies.

DEVELOPMENT AID AND PHILOSOPHY

Bhutan values substantial international aid but places a higher value on the conservation of the Bhutanese way of life, Bhutanese values, and the environment of Bhutan.

In the latter half of the 1990s, Bhutan's total annual budget was about US$150 million. Half of this figure consisted of foreign aid, mostly from Europe, India, and Japan. The most significant expenditure was on the expansion of hydroelectric power. Bhutan appreciates such assistance but will only approve projects that are consistent with traditional values and religion and have no ill affects on the subsistence economy on which most families depend or on the natural resources of Bhutan.

By 2015, or earlier, Bhutan plans to be self-reliant, so that foreign aid will no longer be required to sustain its development program. Much of this will depend on the sale of hydroelectricity. If things go according to plan, the sale of energy to India will more than cover the entire national budget and allow Bhutan to maintain its own pace of development.

Less than 5% of Bhutanese are engaged in commercial activities. The Bhutan Chamber of Commerce and Industry was established in 1980 to promote a more vibrant private sector.

BHUTANESE

THE TERMS "BHUTAN" AND "BHUTANESE" HAVE BEEN APPLIED to the Land of the Thunder Dragon and its people by the outside world since the first non-Bhutanese visitor stepped into the rural paradise. The origin of these terms is certainly Sanskrit, which is the origin of many northern Indian languages and the inspiration for the alphabets of Tibet and Bhutan. The likeliest of several possible interpretations is that "Bhutan" comes from either *bhoottan*, meaning highland, or from *bhotias*, referring to people from the mountains or Tibet.

ETHNIC GROUPS

The population may be broadly divided into three main ethnic groups—Ngalongs in the western and central regions, Sharchops in the east of the country, and Lhotshampas in the southern border areas.

Left: **Bhutanese women building a house in Thimphu. Although men still dominate the politics and economy of Bhutan, development programs since the 1960s have led to increased opportunities for women.**

Opposite: **A grandfather and his grandchild on a street in Thimphu.**

Right: **The slower pace of living facilitates more interaction among family members.**

Opposite: **A Ngalong girl. The Ngalongs are the descendants of Tibetans and the largest ethnic group in Bhutan.**

These basic divisions probably confuse as much as they help when it comes to understanding the differences within the population of Bhutan, who are referred to collectively, in the national language of Dzongkha, as Drukpa. In reality, some of the population and some of the texts on Bhutan consider this term to apply only to the Mongolian groups, while some others feel it applies to those who come from Tibet, i.e. the Ngalongs. There are still others who say the term refers only to those who belong to the Drukpa religious school.

This confusion arises from the close interaction between the secular and the religious in Bhutan's formative history so that language sometimes does not distinguish clearly between secular and religious identities.

NGALONGS

Today's Ngalongs ("NGAR-longs") are descendants of the ninth-century immigrants from Tibet. They arrived, about 100 years or more ago, through the northern passes to settle in the west of what is now Bhutan. The reasons for their migration are lost in time. We know that later migrants from Tibet fled from trouble at home, so unrest might have been a factor in Bhutan's first immigration. But there is no doubt the immigrants were also attracted to the comparatively good farming areas in the uninhabited valleys of western Bhutan. The Ngalongs regard that part of Bhutan west of the Black Mountains, including Thimphu, Paro, and Ha, as their homeland.

The Ngalongs look like their Tibetan ancestors. Their language is also closely related to Tibetan, with some pronunciation and grammatical differences. It is the language of the Ngalongs, known as Dzongkha, that became the national language of Bhutan.

The Ngalongs have for 1,000 years been separated from their neighbors in central Bhutan by the Black Mountains, which tower at 16,410 feet (5,000 m). Today a road twists and turns over the 10,830 feet-high (3,300 m) pass of Pele La, which joins the two parts of the country.

SHARCHOPS

The name Sharchops ("SHAR-khops"), or the alternative Sharchopas, means "people of the east," indicating that they live in eastern and southeastern Bhutan. The environment in the east of Bhutan is less rigorous than in the west since it is warmer and has drier deep valleys. The Sharchops are regarded as the original people of Bhutan or the "first-comers," although where they came from is unknown. House styles vary between the typically large and solid Bhutanese house and more fragile bamboo houses raised on stilts.

The Sharchops are considered to be very religious, and their communities are dotted with small community or family temples. Sharchop women are known for their weaving skills. They work with silk and cotton, and today a good piece of their work, if it is for sale, can cost hundreds of dollars in the open international market.

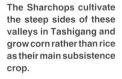

The Sharchops cultivate the steep sides of these valleys in Tashigang and grow corn rather than rice as their main subsistence crop.

LHOTSHAMPAS

The Lhotshampas ("Lhot-SHARM-pahs") of the southern foothills and lowlands are mostly descendants of immigrants from Nepal who came to Bhutan between 1880 and 1960. Studies show that their migration to Bhutan was a continuation of a west-east migration pattern that had existed in Nepal for hundreds of years, largely fueled by overpopulation and scarcity of resources.

Eventually they came to the eastern border of Nepal, which was already occupied by people known as Limbus, who objected to the occupation of their traditional lands. Rather than move south into the disease-infested lowlands of Nepal, the migrants crossed the border into Sikkim and West Bengal and moved further into the mid-level hills of Bhutan's western regions of Ha, Samchi, Chhukha, and Daga, where they cleared the forest and established farms. As their numbers increased, they cleared lands right up to the southern border with India and continued the westward movement across Bhutan.

Most Nepalese settlers are found in southern and southwestern Bhutan. They make up about one-third of the population, speak Nepalese, and most practice Hinduism.

55

LIFESTYLE

BHUTANESE LIFESTYLE IS DETERMINED by isolation, both from outside influence and between parts of Bhutan; the predominance of subsistence farming; and the strong attachment to Tantric Buddhism.

Centuries of isolation means that local society, language, and culture direct the world view of a Bhutanese, and meaningful social relationships are found within his or her own valley. Subsistence farming does not produce any great surpluses that take a farmer to distant markets, so there is little reason to travel long distances. The belief in Buddhism that the Bhutanese share does occasionally prompt pilgrimages to sacred locations. However, for daily religious purposes, a farmer visits his local shrine, where he worships with family and neighbors. The Bhutanese lifestyle is essentially domestic and parochial and, for most people, it has not changed much since the country was unified in the 17th century.

WORKING WAYS

Most of the 85 to 90% of Bhutanese who work on the land are agriculturists. They also keep animals, not for their meat but to pull ploughs and carts, carry harvest produce, and provide milk and wool.

The country's population tends to be congregated in villages on fertile patches of valley land. Hundreds of years of isolation have created close-knit and self-reliant communities, where neighbors often exchange labor and work on each other's land in turn, as well as discuss issues that affect the community as a whole.

Above: **The community spirit is evident in small villages. Here, neighbors come together to help a family build a house.**

Opposite: **Bhutanese are liberal where marriage is concerned. Polygamy is allowed, and divorces are common.**

The most amazing thing about a Bhutanese traditional house is that no nails, screws, or metal hinges are used in its construction. All materials used are locally available.

The roof is typically made of overlapping wooden shingles. The slope of the roof is slight, so large rocks are placed in rows on the shingles to keep them in place. In towns and some villages near a road, wooden shingles have been replaced with corrugated iron sheeting or slate tiles.

Between the ceiling and the roof is a low attic that serves as additional storage space. Besides keeping hay, which is used to feed the animals on the lower floor, the attic also serves to insulate the house.

The wooden front of the house may be carved and painted with religious and folk symbols. Bhutanese believe that they will bring good luck and fertility to the occupants and keep away the bad spirits which spread disharmony and disease.

Before a new house is occupied, it is blessed by monks, and a Buddhist prayer flag is placed on top of the roof. Several other flags may flutter from bamboo poles at the sides of the house.

BIRTH

Most births take place in the home, and any birth, whether it is a boy or a girl, is cause for ceremony and celebration. After a baby is born, a purification ceremony has to be performed in the house on the third day before the child may receive any visitors. Customarily, gifts of eggs, rice, or corn are prepared, and the newborn baby will be given some money for good luck and prosperity.

There is no rush to name the child. The parents often visit one or more reputable abbots or monks to select good luck names. Once the name has been decided, the child's *kyetsi* ("KAI-et-si") or horoscope is determined.

PUBERTY

Bhutanese treat puberty as a natural event, and there is no special rite of passage related to puberty, as in many traditional cultures. Prepubescent sex is socially forbidden, but once puberty has arrived (often as old as 14 or even 15 years of age), sexual relations and marriage in one of its forms are considered normal.

All new mothers will consume a hot alcoholic beverage made with butter and eggs to increase the milk supply. The same drink is served to guests, and everybody is happy and full of good wishes after drinking a few cups.

THE KYETSI

The *kyetsi* horoscope is drawn up with great care, based on the child's birth date according to the Bhutanese lunar calendar. It lists all the rituals the child has to perform throughout his or her life in order to maintain good health and have a good life, as well as additional rituals that are to be performed when the child experiences problems. The *kyetsi* reflects the fatalistic attitude of most Bhutanese but provides a source of psychological comfort when life delivers hard punches.

A Bhutanese marriage does not involve any vows to love, honor, and obey. Sororal polygyny, a rare form of marriage, is practiced in Bhutan, where a man marries two or more sisters. The present king is married to four sisters.

MARRIAGE

The majority of Bhutanese, who cannot afford expensive weddings or do not want a formal wedding, enter marriage gradually—the girl will move in with the boy, and nothing needs to be announced. If the arrangement does not work out, they drift apart or separate. Women as well as men have the right to decide if they wish to continue in a relationship. Society does mildly object to a wife leaving her husband for another man, but social disapproval rarely goes beyond requiring the "other man" to pay a fine to the husband.

Young people today are likely to want their parents' blessing for their union. If it is not given, the couple will present both sides with a *fait accompli*. Nobody would suggest that strangers get married, and children are not obliged to accept the choice of the parents.

A typical lavish wedding begins on an auspicious day and time set by an astrologer. Accompanied by his male friends, the bridegroom fetches the bride from her house and takes her to his house, where members of his family stand in front of the door in welcome, holding a bowl of milk and a bowl of water, symbolizing fertility and prosperity.

A line of monks will bestow ritual blessings on the couple, who exchange cups of alcohol as the sign of the union. Families, neighbors, and friends will present the couple with white scarves to indicate their good wishes and hand over wedding gifts, which are usually pieces of fabric presented in good luck quantities of three, five, or seven. A feast follows, with liberal consumption of alcohol and dancing.

FUNERALS

The funeral is the most important and costly of ceremonies for the Bhutanese, who believe strongly in reincarnation and therefore take serious measures to ensure that a deceased is reborn in the most favorable circumstance.

The lamas are called to the house as soon as possible after death has occurred and read the Book of the Dead. This Book, Tibetan in origin, guides the dead person's spirit through the various stages of *bardo* ("BAR-do"), the state between death and reincarnation.

The body is cremated at an auspicious time chosen by an astrologer, usually three days after death. The corpse, placed in a fetal position, is wrapped in a white cloth, laid on the funeral pyre, and the wood is set alight. Everybody in the locality attends this farewell ceremony, throwing white scarves and paper money into the flames and praying for a good reincarnation. The ashes are usually scattered in the nearest river. Prayer flags are raised to bring merit to the deceased and hasten a good rebirth.

Funeral rites are usually held in the house for seven days. When a child dies during or soon after birth, the elaborate funeral rites are not carried out. Instead the body is left in a field to be eaten by vultures.

RELIGION

BHUTAN IS THE ONLY COUNTRY IN THE WORLD with the Tantric form of Mahayana Buddhism as its official religion. Today freedom of religion is guaranteed in Bhutan, and as part of this freedom, it is forbidden to persuade or force people to change religions, although individuals may change if they wish. About 75% or more of the population are Tantric Buddhists. The remainder includes a large minority of Hindus, mostly in the south, some small pockets of the Bon religion (the original animistic belief system of the Himalayas), and some syncretic religions among noncaste groups in the south.

TANTRIC BUDDHISM

Buddhism, as it is understood and practiced in Bhutan, is considered the final development of the religion's long evolution. The name "Tantric" refers to the Tantras, a large body of esoteric texts that are thought to have been produced between the third and tenth centuries. Tantric Buddhism forms part of the "larger vehicle" (Mahayana) of Buddhist thought, in the sense of recognizing more

scriptures and an enlarged role for the lamas. It includes all the basic truths as set out by the Buddha Gautama. The other main branch of Buddhist thought is called Theravada or Hinayana, meaning the little vehicle, which recognizes only the original Buddhist scriptures. Tantric Buddhism is also referred to in some of the literature as *Vajrayana*, the Diamond Vehicle. It originated in India like all forms of Buddhism but disappeared from India following the Muslim invasions in the 13th century.

Above: **A monk prepares for a ceremony in front of a *thanka* ("TANG-kha") or painting of Guru Rimpoche.**

Opposite: **Young monks take a breather from their studies in front of Thimphu's Dechen Pho-drang School.**

Tantric Buddhism recognizes bodhisattvas ("BOD-hi-sat-vars")—*enlightened beings who have progressed to the point of Nirvana but decline it in order to be reborn and help others toward that goal.*

BUDDHISM: THE SHARED BASIC BELIEFS

All types of Buddhism and all sects agree on the basic principles of the belief system, as given in sermons by Sakyamuni Buddha (also called Gautama) on the India-Nepal border around 560 B.C. These basic tenets are:

THE FOUR NOBLE TRUTHS

1. Human life is full of suffering.
2. People create this suffering because they are afraid to let go—they grasp after the temporary pleasures of life and happiness.
3. If people stop grasping and trying to possess what gives them pleasure and avoid what gives them pain, suffering will cease.
4. Following the Noble Eightfold Path will help people let go and lead eventually to the end of suffering.

THE NOBLE EIGHTFOLD PATH

1. **RIGHT VIEWS**—think positively of the good in oneself and in other people.
2. **RIGHT THOUGHTS**—care for others, be sympathetic and understanding.
3. **RIGHT SPEECH**—do not lie or say hurtful or stupid things.
4. **RIGHT ACTION**—do not kill, injure, or steal.
5. **RIGHT LIVELIHOOD**—in your work do not cheat anyone or cause harm.
6. **RIGHT EFFORT**—make the effort needed to follow the eightfold path.
7. **RIGHT MINDFULNESS**—be aware of your thoughts and actions.
8. **RIGHT CONCENTRATION**—be peaceful in your mind.

THE FIVE PRECEPTS

These are the Buddha's five rules for everyday life:
1. Be sympathetic and helpful to all living things, and do not harm or kill them.
2. Do not steal or take what is not given freely by others, and be generous to the needy.
3. Never take more than you need.
4. Do not tell lies or say bad things about others.
5. Never act thoughtlessly or carelessly.

BELIEFS

The fundamental beliefs of Tantric Buddhism parallel those of Buddhism. The Buddha proclaimed the absence of any god or supreme beings and replaced the idea of deity with the philosophy of cause and effect—that the consequence of actions in previous lives obliges all life forms to reincarnate forever, until and unless the release from the cycle of rebirth is achieved through enlightenment, when all grasping and suffering (which accompanies all existence) is extinguished in the void of Nirvana.

In the case of Tantric Buddhism, great emphasis is placed on the teacher (or lama), whose interaction with laymen is necessary to an understanding of the Tantras, and on ritual practice and meditation as paths towards enlightenment. As such, the recitation of mantras, the turning of prayer wheels, the erection of prayer flags, prostrations to the Buddha, and the creation and use of *mandalas* (paintings on paper and in sand), can help a Bhutanese achieve his real goal in life, which is not to live longer and get richer, but to advance toward enlightenment.

Buddhism is a major source of inspiration for Bhutanese art. *Mandalas*, which are schematized representations of the cosmos in Hindu and Buddhist iconography, are a favorite subject, and they adorn the walls and ceilings of most *dzongs*.

A death dancer frightens off evil spirits at a Harvest Festival in Sakteng.

BON

Bon was an ancient religion that existed throughout the Himalayas before Buddhism arrived in Bhutan in the seventh century. Mostly because Buddhism does not prohibit the holding of two (or more) religions, Bon beliefs and practices became fused with Buddhism.

Certain warlike Bon deities are thought to be predecessors of the pantheon of deities associated with Tantric Buddhism, and some of them are bloodthirsty in appearance. Such "Buddhist gods" take on this form to subdue evil spirits—precisely what the old Bon gods did to help the followers. Likewise, the Bon practice of praying to their gods to bring rain, cure illness, overcome poverty, and obtain objects of desire continues today, although this has nothing to do with Buddhist thought. Prayers are offered to the Buddha, the *bodhisattvas*, and a variety of deities requesting intervention in material life and promising offerings if successful intervention takes place.

Another vestige of the Bon religion is the significance Bhutanese place on mountains and lakes. Some mountains are considered sacred, so man cannot set foot on the higher elevations or stand on the summits without risking dire consequences.

Bhutanese worship the Buddha, Guru Rimpoche, and all the deities of the Tantric and Bon pantheon. Such worship is extended to the religious masters.

DAILY PRACTICE

Bhutanese farmers need no intellectual rationalization of their religion. They are born Buddhist and adopt the beliefs and practices of their family and community. They have a duty to assist and respect monks and religious teachers and to lead life in such a way as to gain merit and thereby be reincarnated at a higher level of consciousness.

Bhutanese adhere strictly to Buddha's commandments, the chief of which is not to kill. They do not hunt or fish or kill their farm animals. However, if such animals die of old age, fall off a cliff, or are on sale at the market when dead, they are eaten. Bhutanese also have a duty to perform daily and special-occasion rituals and to participate in the religious festivals that constantly punctuate Bhutanese life.

Tantric practices require them to make daily prayers and offerings at the altar inside their home, visit temples on special occasions, give to monks, lamas, and monasteries, encourage at least one son to enter monkhood, light butter lamps in homage, make pilgrimages to holy places, turn prayer wheels on every occasion, make appropriately elaborate rituals on the occasion of birth and death, erect prayer flags, and take part in collective prayers.

There are about 7,000 monks in Bhutan today, and they play an important role in the daily lives of people, performing religious ceremonies and preserving traditional scholarship.

THE OFFICIAL RELIGION

The special role religious masters have in Tantric Buddhism has led to many different schools of thought, each following the particular interpretations or teachings of a master. All masters recognize the basic principles of Buddhist dogma, and because of the built-in tolerance of Buddhism, which allows Buddhists to belong to other religions and practice any of the "many paths to Enlightenment," no conflict arises between the schools of thought. Currently the official or national religion of Drukpa (Dragon Sect) coexists with Nyingmapa (Old Sect), which was the sect founded by the revered Guru Rimpoche and is believed by scholars to be the earliest form of Tibetan Tantric Buddhism.

The Drukpa school was founded in Tibet by Tsangpa Gyare Yeshe Dorje (1161–1211), whose teachings were brought to western Bhutan in 1222 by Phajo Drugom Shigpo. The Drukpa school's influence spread throughout the country after Shabdrung Ngawang Namgyal unified the country under a system of government that gave full power to the Drukpas.

THE DIAMOND-THUNDERBOLT

The *dorje* ("DOR-jay"), or the diamond-thunderbolt, looks like a baby's rattle. Four or eight prongs branch out in two directions from the center of an axis, curl around and join together again at either end. It is also known by the Sanskrit term *vajra* ("VAJ-rah"), meaning "diamond."

The diamond-thunderbolt is very symbolic and also the most important of the many ritual objects associated with Tantric Buddhism. The belief is that diamonds and thunderbolts represent purity and indestructibility, and together they represent knowledge and the male element.

To an outsider, some imagination may be needed to see the representation of a diamond and thunderbolt in this ritual object. To a Bhutanese, however, it is evident. In rituals the *dorje* is often combined with a bell known as *drilbu* ("DRILL-boo"), which represents wisdom and the female element. The *dorje* was Guru Rimpoche's weapon; he used it to control demons, convert them, and then made to build temples.

There are at any one time about 250 nuns; the state supports about 50 of them. They live in small communities under the supervision of a monastery. They learn the basic texts and some ritual but rarely take a role as teachers, except to other women.

WISDOM IS A WOMAN

Tantric Buddhism sees knowledge (the body of consciously recognized fact) as male in essence. Wisdom (appropriate use of knowledge) is female. Knowledge by itself is static, and wisdom by itself has no meaning. To progress along the path toward the sublime state of Enlightenment requires union of knowledge and wisdom.

For this reason, Tantric divinities are often represented in sexual union. Just as life cannot continue without man and woman, life (which is suffering) cannot be extinguished without fusing the male and female. Male and female divisions, like all relative truth, cease to exist when their nature is perfectly understood. If this begins to sound a little esoteric, it explains why Tantric Buddhism places emphasis on the interaction between a religious master and his disciple.

Butter sculptures are the Bhutanese alternative to animal sacrifice.

DAGGERS AND SACRIFICES

In Hindu and Bon pre-Buddhist religions, animal sacrifice was practiced. In Buddhism, however, the taking of a life is strictly forbidden. Tantric Buddhism replaces animal sacrifice with sacrificial cakes made of rice dough and butter that are molded into various shapes depending on the preferences of a particular deity. Known as *tormas* ("TOR-mars"), these cakes form part of every ceremony and are placed on the altar in the same way human and animal offerings were made in pre-Buddhist times.

The same procedure is followed for demons. At any ritual of purification where misfortune is blamed on evil spirits or where spiritual protection is essential, sacrificial daggers, known as *phurpa* ("PUR-pah"), are commonly used—not to kill the demons but to liberate them from their evil bodies and send them on the way to a better rebirth.

LAMAS

The term "lama" has a broader meaning than simply "monk." It refers to a religious master and teacher. It is an honorary title of address that indicates knowledge and wisdom about religion, and religious status in society. The title is not in itself inherited but is often transmitted from father to son along with the role of religious teacher. It applies to any of the following:

Gelong ("GE-long") Ordained monks who live in monasteries or *dzongs*, wear a dark red robe, and take the full range of vows and renounce sex and marriage, are called *gelong*. Most enter a monastery at between 6 and 10 years of age, an act that brings great merit to the donor family and provides the boy with what until recently would have been his only chance of an education.

At any one time there are around 7,000 monks in Bhutan, just over 1% of the entire population, or 2% of males. Most of these belong to the official Drukpa sect, but there are also *gelong* of the Nyingmapa. Monks take a range of vows between novice and the fully ordained. In addition to celibacy, they are required to abstain from alcohol, tobacco, and other drugs. While some extremes of long, silent meditation practice are known, they are not the norm. Should they find the vows too demanding, or as more frequently happens, if they wish to leave to get married, they can buy themselves out of their vows. They are then no longer entitled to the title of *gelong* and are known by another title, which nevertheless still carries respect.

Tulku ("TOOL-khoo") Those who can trace their line of descent through reincarnation from a great master (all in the line bear the same name, although they are not linked by blood ties) are known as *tulkus* and are addressed as *rimpoche* (great precious one). Once a man is declared a *tulku*, he remains one whatever he does. Thus, there are *tulkus* fully ordained and *tulkus* who lead a normal family life.

Gomchens ("GOM-chens") *Gomchens* marry, have a family, and go about their daily lives when they are not performing ceremonies for others, usually in return for small payments. They play an important role in isolated villages where no fully ordained monk may be available. Their religious attire is a dark, red cloak that resembles that of a monk. They sometimes wear their hair long in a ponytail. Most, but not all, belong to the Nyingmapa.

LANGUAGE

THERE ARE ALMOST AS MANY LANGUAGES SPOKEN in Bhutan as there are ethnic groups, and often language or dialect differs significantly between neighboring valleys. Given the geographic isolation of many of Bhutan's highland villages, it is not surprising that a number of different dialects have survived. None of the languages had a written form until the 20th century, and the language of the monasteries, and therefore of education, was classical Tibetan, known as Choeke *("CHO-kay")*.

Today the national language is Dzongkha ("DZONG-kha"), which has been written using the Choeke script only since the 1960s. English is widely used, particularly in the educational system. Ngalopkha, also derived from Tibetan, is spoken in western Bhutan. Sharchopkha, an Indo-Mongolian language, is the dominant language in eastern Bhutan. Nepali is spoken in the south.

Left: **By promoting the national language of Dzongkha, the Bhutanese government hopes to enhance its national integration.**

Opposite: **The Kuensel, a weekly newspaper owned by the government, is the only newspaper in the country.**

Given the geographic isolation of many villages, it is not surprising that a number of different dialects have survived.

CHOEKE

Choeke was the lingua franca of the religious authorities of a huge area that stretched from Mongolia and Tibet to the Himalayan kingdoms of Bhutan, Ladakh, Nepal, and Sikkim. Classified linguistically as Tibeto-Burman, Choeke is thought to have been invented in the seventh century and was in widespread use by the eighth century. As a written system for Classical Tibetan, it represents an adaptation of a seventh-century alphabet from Northern India which is no longer in use. It reads from left to right, has 30 consonants and four vowels. Since Tibetan, like Dzongkha, is a two-tone language, the correct pronunciation of a syllable required memorization, which was the normal way of learning in the monasteries.

LANGUAGES OF BHUTAN

Four main language groups exist—Dzongkha in the west and north; Bumthangkha in the central region; Sharchopkha in the east; and Nepali

in the south. The first three of these each have regional dialects, and the fourth is a common language spoken by various groups that migrated to Bhutan from Nepal in early 20th century. Some of these groups have their own languages, which are not dialects of Nepali. The Tamang, for example, live in the south and can speak Nepali as well as Tamang, a language nearer to Tibetan and Dzongkha than Nepali.

DZONGKHA

The official language, Dzongkha, is the mother tongue of the Ngalong people of the Thimphu valley and Western Bhutan. English was used mainly in the south, where Dzongkha was little known until its use expanded in schools in the 1990s. Gradually Dzongkha spread throughout the country and became the undisputed national language. Although English is the primary medium of instruction in all schools, Dzongkha continues to be taught. The government sees the national language as a means to preserve Bhutan's culture and strengthen its national identity.

Both English and Dzongkha are used on signboards, posters, and advertisements across the country.

VERBAL COMMUNICATION

As in any language, Dzongkha or the other languages spoken in Bhutan, including English, have usages that are characteristic to the country. In Bhutan it is always important to show respect to the person being addressed, so it is considered rude to speak too loudly and polite to use the particle *la* at the end of a phrase or sentence, particularly an order, to soften the tone. This use of the *la*-particle is often carried over into English—as in "Shut the door-*la.*"

NONVERBAL COMMUNICATION

As elsewhere in South and Southeast Asia, body language is as important as words in expressing respect and good manners. Heads are sacred, and feet are considered to be the dirtiest part of the body. Whether sitting in a modern armchair or on the floor, feet should be tucked out of the way and should not point at anyone, and shoes are removed when visiting a home or a temple.

Homage is shown to very important religious figures in the same way as to the Buddha, with three full prostrations and the prostrator's head placed at the level of the religious master's feet.

Demonstrating good manners is important for both host and guest when invitations are made to visit the home. (Those procedures are set down in the section on Food.)

SAYING NO

Bhutanese consider a clear "no" to be too blunt for good manners. Thus, they have perfected various ways of saying yes, which vary from full agreement, through "I'm not sure," to the full meaning of no, which is likely to be expressed with nothing stronger than "perhaps."

EXCHANGING PRESENTS

Bhutanese exchange presents as a form of etiquette. Those receiving a gift do not open it until they are alone. To do otherwise would be more than bad manners, it would imply that the recipient wants more of the same. Gifts between equals are always reciprocated. However, when a gift is of significant value and comes from a person of high status, it is reciprocated with loyalty and service rather than with a gift.

At important events, such as birth, marriage, getting a good job or an award, and going abroad, the traditional present is cloth. The status of the donor would be evident in the number of pieces given. Money put in an envelope may be used as a substitute, along with the obligatory white scarf. The symbolic value of the scarf is of vital importance when visiting *dzongs*, monasteries, or taking part in official ceremonies.

The act of giving a white scarf speaks louder than words and is a must for every Bhutanese at any important event. These scarves are recycled until they show signs of wear and tear.

NAMES

A few weeks after a baby is born, the parents seek out a monk to name the child. The monk gives two names to every child, whether girl or boy. Very few Bhutanese names are gender-specific; therefore it is usually impossible to tell the gender of a person by looking at his or her name without a title.

Except for the royal family, Bhutanese have only the names given by a religious person. There are no family names. The two given names will be different, and there is no fixed position for a name. Dorji, for example, can be a person's first or second name. It is normal to address a person by first name or by both names, but not by second name alone.

The system of naming is simple in Bhutan, with only 50 non-gender-specific names to choose from. There are no family names.

There are only some 50 names in existence, and almost all of them originate from Tibetan. Among the most common names are Dorji and Wangchuck, the two family names of Bhutanese royalty, which can be used by anybody as personal names without in any way indicating a royal link. Women keep their names after marriage.

People of Nepali ancestry in the south also do not have family names. If they are caste-Hindus, however, they use one of the names belonging to their caste group, and this is passed on within the family. Noncaste Nepali-origin people generally use their ethnic name in place of a family name—all Rais are called Rai; Limbus are called Limbu (or its equivalent); Tamangs are called Tamang; and Gurungs are called Gurung.

Today Bhutanese parents have to register the birth of their child at the district office.

TITLES

Any Bhutanese of high status is addressed by his or her title, followed by first name or both names.

Dasho refers to a male member of the royal family, to those who have been honored by the king with the red scarf, and by polite extension to senior government officials.

Ashi is used with a female member of the royal family.

Lyonpo is reserved for ministers.

Lopon is used when speaking to a senior monk.

Rimpoche is used when addressing a reincarnated lama; and

Anim when speaking to a nun.

Aap is used when speaking to a man (equal);

Busu for a boy;

Am is for an older woman; and

Bum for a girl.

Aapa, Ama, Alou, Bumo, are used respectively for men, women, boys, and girls of unknown name, for instance, restaurant staff.

ARTS

BHUTANESE ART IS CHARACTERIZED BY CONFORMITY IN FORM, religious or folk content, and significant Tibetan influence. Form and content have remained practically unchanged over hundreds of years, making art literally timeless. The characteristic theme of most representational art, dance-drama, and music is the eternal battle between good and evil. Art work is almost always anonymous, although significant sponsors are often named. Often a work of art is a collective achievement of several artists working together, either all at once, or one after the other. It may be a group of people decorating the front of a house with carvings and paintings, two monks painting a *mandala*, a troop of monks dancing and playing music, or apprentices roughing out the work for the master to add the finishing touches.

The first School of Bhutanese Arts and Crafts was opened in 1680 under the orders of Shabdrung Ngawang Namygal, who had probably been dead for 31 years at the time!

Left: **Dancing in masks is frequent during religious festivals in Bhutan.**

Opposite: **A Bhutanese craftsman sells his work in the market.**

Above: **Painted masks are popular tourist souvenirs.**

Opposite: **Buddhist monks unveil a giant** *thanka* **of Guru Rimpoche during a** *tsechu* **festival.**

PAINTING

Bhutanese religious painting has kept its form over many centuries, and there is very little room for individual expression. There has, however, been a certain development. Style has become more ornate as Chinese influences entered from the 17th century. Gold paint is lavishly applied, and Chinese landscapes are common subjects. Colors are traditionally mixed from natural materials—earth, minerals, and vegetable matter— although recently chemical dyes have been introduced. Brushes continue to be made from animal hair tied to twigs of wood. Colors are applied in a set order and with thought as to what they represent.

Wall paintings and *thankas* are the most spectacular examples of Bhutanese painting. A wall painting in a monastery is likely to be sponsored by a lay person who often specifies the main person or deity and the scene to be painted, leaving little room for spontaneity. The paint may be applied directly to sanded, pressed mud or onto thin layers of cloth glued to the wall with a paste that repels insects.

Before any painting begins, the composition is sketched on the wall with great care. Proportions must be correct. Sometimes a master artist makes the preparations, leaves the painting to apprentices, and then returns to apply the finishing touches. If there is a name associated with the work, it will be that of the sponsor or *jinda* ("JIN-dar"), not the artist or artists. The inner walls of *dzongs* and temples or *ihakhangs* ("i-HAK-khang") are usually covered with such paintings. Only a few have survived across the centuries because of the habit of repainting over the same walls, which is regarded as an act of merit.

A *thangka* is a cotton cloth stretched on a wooden frame, primed with lime and glue, and painted. The imagery might represent a Buddha, a deity, or the geometric *mandala*. Even a small *thangka* can take many days to complete, with very fine lines and gilding. Taken from its frame, the *thangka* is mounted with brocade borders and then affixed with wooden sticks at the top and bottom to allow hanging. When not on show, a *thangka* is usually rolled up and protected from the light.

Some very large thangkas called thondrols ("TONG-drols") are kept in the dzong and displayed briefly on the walls during a tsechu. By viewing them, people can be magically cleansed of their sins.

DZONGS

The first system of defensive fortresses known as *dzongs* was put into place in the 17th century by the remarkable Shabdrung Ngawang Namgyal, unifier of Bhutan. They played a role in repulsing the Tibetan and Mongolian invasions, and arms captured over three centuries ago are still kept as trophies in the *dzongs*. The defensive *dzongs* contained everything important that an attacker might want to possess or destroy—the ruling families, the administrative offices and records, the monastery, a large granary, and systems of access to underground water. In the event of attack, the *dzong* could also provide sanctuary to many of the farmers in the district.

The Punakha Dzong in Thimphu is the oldest monastery in Bhutan.

The oldest *dzongs* are built in a style reflecting the political philosophy of the time and region. In some *dzongs* the walls surround a large courtyard from which a central commanding tower rises up above the outer walls, monks' quarters, and administrative offices. In others the central tower cuts the *dzong* into two equal parts and two courtyards—one owned by the clergy, the other by the temporal authority. Other *dzongs* follow neither of these patterns and are built to accommodate the rugged terrain on which they stand.

The inside walls of *dzongs* and monasteries and the great doors are richly decorated with paintings and slate engravings, and on festive days are the backdrop for the artistic treasures brought out for short periods on special occasions. Like the traditional houses found in any Bhutanese village, *dzongs* and monasteries are constructed without the use of nails or metal hinges. With their painted frescoes of protective deities, their grandeur and majesty, *dzongs* encapsulate Bhutanese culture. Any Bhutanese entering this environment becomes a part of it, aided in this by the wearing of the national costume and the scarf.

A *dzong* in Paro. While the outside of the *dzong* presents a stony face to the world, the inside walls are traced with wooden balconies and galleries faced with richly colored, painted wood.

A traditional weaver's loom in Bumthang. Eastern Bhutan is well known for its stunning, hand-loomed textiles.

WEAVING

Bhutanese textiles have only recently reached the outside world and have made such an impression that demand greatly outstrips supply, sending prices sky rocketing. The quality of weaving is among the world's highest. For a single excellent piece of cloth of blanket length, a price exceeding twice the Bhutanese per capita income would not be unusual. Nevertheless, the Bhutanese have not forsaken the land to go into commercial cloth production; weaving remains a spare-time activity. With the time available, each male member of the family is assured a beautiful *gho* ("GOH") and the female member a *kira* ("KI-rah"). There is little thought of selling to a tiny tourist market that as yet is unseen by most Bhutanese.

Cloth is highly valued in Bhutan. Traditional gifts at funerals and other occasions are pieces of cloth, given in uneven numbers. The more cloth given, the higher the status of the giver. Status has a lot to do with weaving. Bhutanese will use part of their tiny annual income to buy silk from Vietnam, China, or India that can be woven together with cotton thread to make a richer cloth. The most remarkable weaving uses a technique of supplementary threads that makes the pattern stand out. Natural dyes are still in use. Various types of loom exist in Bhutan; one of the most common is the portable backstrap loom, which hangs from the wall of a house and loops around the back of the weaver. This loom is found throughout Asia. Its disadvantage is that it can only produce narrow bands of cloth. Therefore, to produce a single *kira* or a blanket for one person requires three widths, which are sewn together.

Almost all of Bhutan's weavers are female. The traditional designs for *gho* and *kira* are passed from mother to daughter and vary little. Stripes are usual and are worn vertically by men and horizontally by women. On heavier woolen clothing, checked patterns are common, and this design is worn by both men and women. The intricacy of design, the quality of the threads, the craftsmanship, and the cleanliness of a *gho* and *kira* reflect the status of a family.

WEARING A *GHO* AND *KIRA*

The male *gho* very much resembles a bath robe with the cuffs turned back. The left front side is worn across the right, and the waist is folded until the hemline comes up to the knees before being secured by a woven belt called a *kera*.

The female *kira* reaches to the ankles. It is always worn over a long undershirt. The *kira* is a rectangle piece of cloth draped around the back and brought under the arms and across the breasts so that the folds fasten at the left shoulder. The second fold crosses the first and fastens at the right shoulder. Fastening is by means of small silver brooches called *koma* ("KOH-mah"). The folds are kept in place at the waist by a woven *kera*.

LEISURE

THE GREAT MAJORITY OF BHUTANESE lead full working lives in the fields and pastures. Farming methods are primitive, and the use of labor-saving devices is limited. Although there are good and bad harvests, the average family produces sufficient food to meet its own needs, with a little surplus to bring in extra income.

Times of the year that are not labor-intensive are usually given over to house repair, weaving cloth and baskets, and doing the many jobs that are essential if the farm and family are to get by in the year ahead. It is during these times that couples, if they have decided to announce their union to the community, get married; young boys enter the monastery, with the village to see them off; and people make merit, attending the temple, donating to the monks and the monastery, and sponsoring and attending *tsechu* festivities.

Left: **Besides being a medium of Buddhist teaching,** *tsechus* **are huge social gatherings, drawing a crowd of locals and tourists.**

Opposite: **Volleyball is a recent import to Bhutan.**

Cheerleaders for archery competitions are allowed to distract the opposing team by shouting rude comments.

ARCHERY

Datse ("DAT-say"), or archery, is Bhutan's national sport and a high-profile activity. The country is well known for its level of skill in archery, and apart from the southern areas, almost every village and *dzong* in the country has a place set aside for the activity. No festivity is complete without an archery match, and each match is accompanied by its cheerleading teams and high excitement.

Women follow the match every bit as much as men. Dressed in their finest *kiras*, they cheer and encourage their team, dancing and singing before the competition and during intervals. They are, however, not included in competitive teams, although some all-women competitions are beginning to appear.

Believing that sleeping with a woman will drain the force, an archery team will sometimes sleep in a monastery or in a special accommodation at the *dzong* before the competition. They guard their equipment carefully, make offerings to the deities, and take special care that no woman touches a bow, which would take away its spring. A popular tournament involves two teams taking turns to shoot at wooden targets over a course of 360 feet (120 m).

Today many archers use high-tech imported bows, which are far more powerful and accurate than the traditional bamboo bows. Since the two bows cannot compete on equal terms, there are now two annual tournaments each year—one for traditional bows and one for modern bows. It is now considered only a matter of time before Bhutan fields an Olympic medal-winning team.

FOOTBALL

Football of the British variety, or soccer, is played throughout the summer, usually in the evenings despite the monsoon rains. Competition teams often consist of senior schoolboys. It is very much a local observer sport. Although the Bhutanese soccer teams compete with neighboring countries, the sport is limited to towns and larger centers of population and has yet to gain the enthusiastic following of archery.

THROWING STONES

Since archery is forbidden to monks, monasteries have discovered alternative games and competitions. *Dego* ("DEH-goh") is played with round, smooth stones. A small stick is stuck in the ground, and competitors take turns to throw their stones to land as near to the stick as possible. *Pundo* ("PUN-do"), similar to shotput, is played by monks and laymen. A large stone is thrown from the shoulder, and the longest throw wins.

CINEMAS

There are five widely separated cinemas in Bhutan—one in Thimphu, two in the border town of Phuntsholing, one in Samchi, and one in Samdrup Jongkar. All of them show Hindi movies and are popular. Outside of these urban centers, many Bhutanese have never seen a film.

NIGHTCLUBS AND DRINKING PLACES

There are a few establishments in Thimphu and Paro that might be called nightclubs. They play loud music and offer little else. More common are small shops where men sit to drink Bhutan's wide variety of home-produced rum, gin, whiskey, brandy, and occasional cheap beer imported from India. Such shops usually double as carom parlors, and this Indian game of flicked, checker-like pieces enjoys immense popularity.

STORYTELLING

In the absence of a literary tradition outside of the sacred scriptures, the heroes and myths of Bhutan are kept alive for each new generation by dancers and storytellers. Storytelling is an amateur activity that takes place most frequently between generations of the same family. It also enters into the education provided in the monasteries and in schools, since much Bhutanese history is indistinguishable from myth, particularly the exploits of Guru Rimpoche and Shabdrung Ngawang Namgyal, who followed the deity Yeshey Goenpo (who was in the form of a raven at the time) to find the way to Bhutan. Ngawang Namgyal unified Bhutan, then spent 54 years meditating, during which he is credited with repulsing attacks from Tibet and setting up an art and handicrafts school.

Sometimes truth is stranger than fiction. Bhutan's national flower, the blue poppy, was dismissed as a myth by non-Bhutanese prior to its discovery by an English botanist in 1933. It remains rare but photographs do exist. Another instance where myth and reality converge is the yeti ("YET-ti"), the abominable snowman. Bhutanese claim to have seen it, however foreign expeditions aiming to track it have been unsuccessful.

Today new sports are gaining in favor; basketball and taekwondo in particular are very popular. While women can participate in sports, they are more often spectators.

THE ABOMINABLE SNOWMAN

Bhutanese farmers believe three types of yeti exist. One is large, docile, and nonviolent. Another is a savage carnivore, five-feet tall (1.5 m) with long hair and Neanderthal looks, while the third one is small, shy, and shaggy-haired. All three leave their footprints at altitudes of 16,410 to 26,256 feet (5,000 to 8,000 m) and have a strong, pungent smell. Some scientists consider it possible that a species of mountain gorilla could survive in the remote heights, particularly if it had adapted its eating habits to what is available, particularly yak meat, but none of the expeditions to track down a yeti has been successful. The yeti is pictured in old Bhutanese and Tibetan manuscripts and murals and has recently been honored in Bhutan by five designs of stamps bearing its image.

FESTIVALS

MOST OF THE IMPORTANT FESTIVALS AND EVENTS in Bhutan are scheduled according to the Bhutanese calendar; very few dates commemorating significant events are fixed on the Western calendar. Those that are include Bhutan's National Day on December 17, which is the date the monarchy was established in 1907; the king's Birthday on November 11; and Coronation Day on June 2, which commemorates the day in 1974 when King Jigme Singye Wangchuck came to the throne.

Translating the Bhutanese calendar into the Western calendar is complicated, and finding the most auspicious time for an event is important. Even after astrologers have intervened and local differences have been accounted for, it is difficult to fix a date except in a broad band, which may be two to four weeks in the case of *tsechu* festivals and as much as two months for Losar ("LOH-sar"), the New Year.

TSECHU SCHEDULES FOR 2000/2001

Punakha Dromche	- February 10 to 15, Punakha
Chorten Kora	- February 19 and March 6, Trashigang
Paro Tsechu	- March 17 to 21, Paro
Ura Tsechu	- April 15 to 18, Bumthang
Kurjey Tsechu	- July 11, Bumthang
Thimphu Tsechu	- October 6 to 8, Thimphu
Wangdi Tsechu	- October 5 to 7, Wangdi
Tamshingphala Choepa	- October 8 to 10, Bumthang
Tangbi Mani	- October 13 to 15, Bumthang
Jambay Lhakhang	- November 11 to 14, Bumthang
Jaker Tsechu	- November 11, Bumthang
Mongar Tsechu	- December 3 to 6, Mongar
Trashigang Tsechu	- December 4 to 7, Trashigang
Trongsa Tsechu	- January 3 to 7, 2001, Trongsa
Lhuntse Tsechu	- January 3 to 7, 2001, Lhuntse

The few Bhutanese who do celebrate individual birthdays use the Western calendar. Otherwise everybody has a collective birthday on Losar, which falls some time between January and March. Bhutanese count the time in the mother's womb as part of the life cycle and count themselves one year old the moment they are born.

Opposite: **The sound of long horns, which accompany the low chanting of monks, is an integral part of Bhutanese music.**

Southerners of Nepali-immigrant origin celebrate Nepali New Year on the new moon in April instead of Losar. There are also regional "New Years" that correspond to the local end of the harvest season (November-December) or, in the east, to the winter solstice at the beginning of January.

Fortunately dates of festivals are now published on the Internet and regularly updated as changes are made for one reason or another. An example of the Internet schedule for the year 2000 is given on the previous page. The dates will not be the same in years to come.

Attendance by the public at any official festival, such as a *tsechu*, is not obligatory, but none would want to be left out. Bhutanese working away from home during one of these important religious festivals will make every effort to return and attend.

THE BHUTANESE CALENDAR

The Bhutanese calendar is based on the Tibetan calendar, which is in turn based on the Chinese calendar. The divergence between Tibet and Bhutan goes back to the 17th century when a Bhutanese scholar, Pema Karpo, devised a new way of working out the time. Tibet did not go along with the innovations.

Under the Pema Karpo system, which remains the official Bhutanese system, each month has 30 days. Years are named after 12 animals and five elements, each animal taking on a different element in rotation. For instance, the year 2000 was the year of the Iron Dragon; 1988 was the year of the Earth Dragon; 1976 was the year of the Fire Dragon; 1964 was the year of the Wood Dragon; and 1952 was the year of the Water Dragon.

The 12 animals, in consecutive order are—dragon, serpent, horse, sheep, monkey, hen, dog, pig, mouse, ox, tiger, and hare.

In each 30-day month, some days are auspicious, namely full moon days and the 4th, which was the day the Buddha set out his religious principles. Significant events are set for auspicious days, and astrologers are quite happy to add or skip a day, or even a month for that matter, to make an event fall on a good day.

THE TSECHU

The *tsechu* is a festival held in each *dzong* and some monasteries, usually, but not necessarily, on the 10th of the Bhutanese month. Every *tsechu* is dedicated to Guru Rimpoche, the Second Buddha, and includes dance dramas that illustrate his life.

Celebrated for three to five days, the center of the festival is always the same—the performance of elaborately costumed religious dances known as *chham*, which depict episodes from Guru Rimpoche's life and moral stories from Bhutanese history and mythology. The religious basis of events still allows plenty of secular additions and trimmings. Folk dances, largely performed by young women, present refreshing interludes between the set pieces, and *atsaras* ("AT-sar-ras") or clowns openly mimic the more serious of the monks in their ritualized dances.

Tsechu means "10th day," and celebrations are held then because Guru Rimpoche performed all of his magical miracles on the 10th of the month.

Bhutanese dressed in colorful, traditional *kira* in front of a tea shop during a *tsechu* in Wangi.

MOCKING RELIGION

The *atsaras* present a "rite of reversal," reinforcing the message of the formal drama by behaving in a way that would normally be unacceptable in Bhutanese society. Only an *atsara* in the circumstances of a *tsechu* can make fun of religion and its monks. The *atsara* perform in a deliberately outrageous way, wearing masks with long red noses, making innuendos, and telling jokes that ridicule at the *tsechus*.

The entertainment extends outside the *dzong* with fairs and archery competitions, each team with its following of female cheerleaders. Secular songs and dances by both sexes provide opportunities for people to interact on an informal basis. People wear their finest clothes and jewelry, eat the best food, and drink plenty of alcohol. Everybody gains merit simply by attendance, although some are considered to gain a bit more because they are contributing to the cost. It is also a social opportunity to meet old friends and perhaps make some new ones from among those who live in distant villages. There is much drinking, some gambling, and more than a little flirting. Many marriages have their beginnings at the *tsechus*.

DROMCHE

Besides the *tsechus*, a few of the more important *dzongs*, like Thimphu, Paro, and Punakha, will stage a second large festival called a *dromche*

("DROM-chay"). Similar to a *tsechu*, these are dedicated to the protective deities of the Drukpas. Not every *dzong* can sponsor a Dromche every year. Probably the best known and most spectacular is that of Punakha, which always concludes with a great procession that reenacts episodes from the war with Tibet in the 17th century.

LOSAR

Gyelpo Losar, the Bhutanese New Year, should correspond to the new moon in February, although very often it does not. It is a secular festival with no great communal festivities to prepare, and there is no pragmatic need to fix the date before agreement has emerged on the most auspicious day for it. The result is that different parts of the country can celebrate at different times. It is a relatively quiet affair, with archery contests similar to any holiday. For most people Losar is a time for the family to come together, worship the deity of choice or of the region, and eat and drink.

SECULAR FESTIVALS

In addition to Losar and local festivals peculiar to a region or an area, there are two important secular festivals where the national identity takes priority—National Day on December 17, which celebrates the beginning of the Wangchuck monarchy; and the King's Birthday on November 11. These are celebrated throughout the kingdom with parades and dances in which schoolchildren play the central roles.

A lama performing the Black Hat Dance to subdue evil during a *tsechu*.

FOOD

BHUTAN IS KNOWN FOR THE BEAUTY of its landscape, the friendliness and hospitality of its people, the magnificent architecture of its *dzongs*, and its colorful and ancient festivities. Cuisine is not one of its attractions.

The fact that Bhutanese villagers got the inspiration for one of their staple dishes from an Englishman is perhaps comment enough on the subject. This Englishman traveled in Bhutan in the 18th century and lived on a diet of boiled rice and potatoes; many farmers exist on pretty much the same daily lunch, to which the essential Bhutanese ingredient of chilies is added. Chilies were pretty well the only seasoning until the 1950s, when garlic, onions, and ginger—which were used daily throughout Asia for centuries—were introduced to Bhutan and very quickly spread throughout the kingdom. While the average diet may appear uninspiring to a non-Bhutanese, the population of Bhutan is generally well fed.

Left: **Bhutanese in the Paro Valley dry home-grown chilies on rooftops.**

Opposite: **Villagers and urban dwellers converge at the weekend market in Thimphu to shop for the best bargains.**

A Bhutanese preparing food in the kitchen.

PREPARATION

The average Bhutanese kitchen is as uncomplicated as the diet. Metal pots, a frying wok, a tripod to hold them above the flames (or in its absence some well-placed rocks), and a long knife to chop firewood gathered from the fallen debris of the tree, and the cooking place is ready. The kitchen and fire is normally inside the house, except in the south where it is attached to the main house. In towns and more accessible areas, wood-burning stoves are sometimes found. These are more economical on firewood, safer, and give a more controlled heat. Like all imports from India, however, they are expensive for the average Bhutanese.

Stews are popular and easy to cook in a Bhutanese kitchen. Cheese is melted, vegetables and meat are thrown in, and water is added to a level depending on the number of servings. Usually, but not always, the women do the cooking. Stews may be served in their cooking pots unless a special occasion calls for the distribution of plates. They are placed on the floor next to mounds of rice.

TYPICAL DISHES

Phagshaphu Next to *emadatse* ("YEE-mah-dat-say"), this is the dish most likely to tempt a Bhutanese. Strips of dried pork fat are stewed with radishes or turnips and plenty of dried chilies.

Gondomaru Scrambled eggs cooked in butter.

Noshahuentsu Stewed pork with spinach.

Phagshaphintshom Pork in rice noodles.

Bjashamaru Chicken stewed in garlic and butter sauce.

Momos This Tibetan dish is found throughout the Himalayas. These small, steamed dumplings are filled with meat or cheese.

Tsampa Another Tibetan dish, in which barley flour is mixed with salt and butter, kneaded into a paste and roasted.

Daal-baat Rice with lentils and side-vegetables, some pickles, and curry—the basic meal of the southerners and the Nepalese. It is available in hotels that cater to Indians and is quite popular with the central and northern Bhutanese who have tried it.

Religious strictures against taking a life restrict the variety in the cuisine, but few Bhutanese are fully vegetarian. This includes monks, who eat the same staple food as any other Bhutanese.

A mother feeds her monk son. Rice is picked up with the right hand, molded into a ball, dipped into a soup, and then placed in the mouth.

STAPLES

The Bhutanese eat an enormous quantity of rice and comparatively little else with it. There is a preference for red rice, although both red and white rice are often eaten together. Gradually rice is becoming the staple of the entire country. In villages situated at high altitudes, however, rice will not grow. Instead, wheat and buckwheat are made into pancakes and noodles and served with dried, crushed kernels of corn. Some barley and millet are also eaten, although this is less popular than rice. Rice is usually unpolished and thereby retains its vitamins. Potatoes are eaten often enough to merit inclusion as a staple, but they are seen as a vegetable and usually cooked in the stew.

When traveling or working long hours in the fields, farmers carry a covered basket of *zow* ("ZOW"), rice that is boiled and then fried.

MEAT AND FISH

Most dried meat and fish sold in the market comes from India (including beef). There are no slaughterhouses in Bhutan and few refrigerated storage centers. None of the trucks bringing meat and fish from India is refrigerated, which accounts for the preference for dried foods. Most of the yak meat and pork is from Bhutan, and these animals are presumed to have met with an accident or died of old age. Wags say that considering how few vehicles there are in Bhutan, an extraordinary number of animals die in car accidents.

Most daily stews contain a bone or two with some meat on it, enough to prevent the Bhutanese diet from being totally vegetarian and to give a taste to the stew. On special occasions Bhutanese serve squares of pig fat. This appears to contain its own preservative and is said to be full of energy.

Religious strictures against killing limit the amount of meat that finds its way into the Bhutanese kitchen.

117

VEGETABLES

Bhutanese grow and eat potatoes, mushrooms, asparagus, and some seasonal, green leafy vegetables. These are supplemented with food products collected from the paths and forests on the way to and from the fields—bamboo shoots, mushrooms, taro, yams, sweet potatoes, wild bananas, and river weeds. During the monsoon months, when forest foods are plentiful and delivery of Indian meat to remote areas is difficult because of the rain, the diet consists mainly of vegetables.

Chilies are considered to be a vegetable and are prepared the same way. The national dish, *emadatse* ("YEE-mah-dat-say"), is made entirely of hot, green chilies in a sauce of fresh, melted cheese.

Vegetables are an integral part of the Bhutanese diet because of the limited meat supply and a lack of cold storage facilities.

SNACKS

Bhutanese do not eat dessert after a meal but have a variety of snack foods to present to guests or to sell in the small shops. *Kabze* or fritters are sold at festivals. *Sip* is flattened rice cakes. *Gegasip* are flattened corn cakes. These are often dipped in sweet tea and eaten for breakfast. More fruit is now grown for export, and some of it finds its way into the diet of those who live at higher altitudes. Fruit is more likely to be eaten as a snack rather than incorporated into meals.

Milk is rarely drunk but is churned into butter and cheese. Small, soft cheeses are not eaten as a snack but are used in sauces. *Churpi*, on the other hand, is a popular between-meals plaything for the teeth.

CHURPI

Churpi ("CHOOR-pi") is sold in the form of small yellow cubes. Made of yak milk, this cheese is so hard it can be repeatedly hit with a hammer and still keep its small, square shape. It is held in the mouth for hours, being moved around rather than chewed. It never softens and only gradually dissolves away. *Churpi* has a distinctive taste. It gets the saliva flowing and is said to keep hunger at bay with zero calories.

Bhutanese men sell cold drinks and popcorn during a *tsechu*.

DRINKS

Tea is widely consumed, and there are two popular kinds—*seudja*, which is tea churned with salt and butter, and *nadja*, Indian style tea brewed with milk and sugar. Coffee is rare even in towns. Next to tea and water, alcohol is the most common drink. Alcoholic beverages that are made and sold in Bhutan cover a full range—whiskey, gin, rum, vodka, and brandy. These are also exported to other countries. Beer is imported from India and is sold at a lower price than in its country of origin. Regionally cider is distilled from apples, and peach and apple brandies are also produced.

Drinking alcohol is widely incorporated into rituals and festivals, and the most common marriage ceremony is a simple exchange of glasses of wine.

PLAYING THE HOST

The host must offer a guest tea or alcohol. The guest must take at least a sip or lift the cup a couple of times to the lips, even if he or she does not drink. A first refusal will simply be taken as good manners—meaning that the guest should not pounce on the beverage—and the host is expected to make the offer again. The guest should ideally leave the drink until the host invites the guest with a small touch on the cup or saucer.

If a meal is to be served, alcoholic drinks with snacks will be served one or two hours ahead of the meal. Guests of high status visiting a humble family are likely to be received in the "chapel"—often the best room in the house—with the images of deities around to reflect the elevated status of the guests. When dinner is served, the host may not eat with his guests but simply serve them. Immediately after the meal, the guest puts down his plate and leaves quickly. To hang around would be seen as bad manners.

AIIMA DATCHI

1 onion, sliced
garlic, several cloves
green chilies, split
3 oz (100 grams) cheddar cheese, grated
one tablespoon of flour
two cups of stock
one tablespoon butter, cut into dice
Mix the cheese with the flour. Then cook the onion, garlic, and chilies with stock till tender. Season with salt. Sprinkle half the cheese and flour mixture, cooking for one minute till the gravy thickens. Add the remaining mixture and butter, then cover and turn off the heat. Leave it for 5 to 7 minutes, then serve with plain, steamed rice.
(Recipe by Brian Whyte of Himalayan Hill Treks)

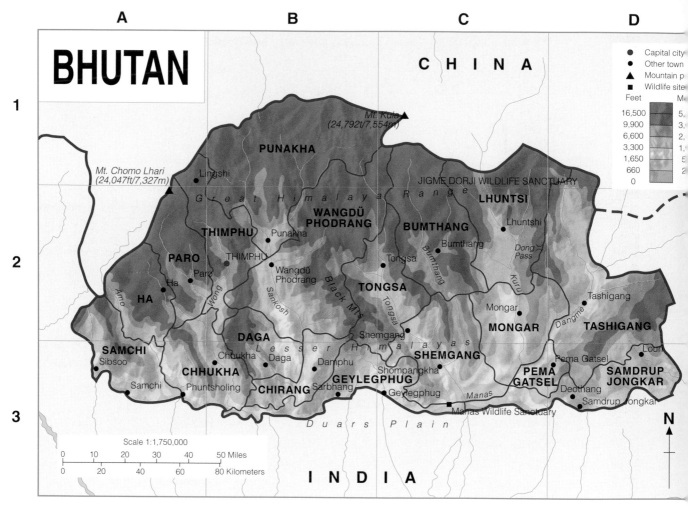

BHUTAN

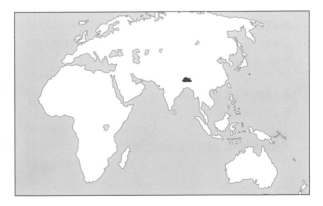

BIBLIOGRAPHY

Aris, M. *Bhutan: The Early History of a Himalayan Kingdom.* Warminster, United Kingdom: Serindia (Publisher), 1979.

Armington, S. *Bhutan.* Oakland, United States: Lonely Planet Publications, 1998.

Kuensel (English and Nepali language newspaper). Thimphu, Bhutan.

Pommaret, F. *Introduction to Bhutan.* Hong Kong: The Guidebook Company Limited, 1990.

http://www.bootan.com

http://www.odci.gov/cia/publications/factbook/geos/bt.html

http://www.tashidelek.com

INDEX

INDEX

INDEX

PICTURE CREDITS
Alison Wright: 18, 32, 89, 96, 111, 114, 119
Christine Osborne Pictures/Ann Cook: 38, 40, 41, 53, 64, 37, 98, 104, 97, 123
Christine Osborne Pictures/Julian Worker: 17
Earl & Nazima Kowall: 15, 16, 116
Earl Kowall: 6, 47, 49, 78, 103
Focus Team: 5, 19, 30, 36, 39, 42, 45, 50, 73, 76, 80, 82, 83, 86, 88, 92, 94, 100, 112, 117, 118
HBL Network: 13
Hulton Getty Picture Library: 28, 33, 34, 35, 60, 66, 67, 69, 91, 95
Hutchison Library: 8, 20, 31, 48, 54, 57, 62, 65, 74, 75, 79, 101, 109
John R. Jones: 3, 21, 22, 25, 55, 61, 68
Nazima Kowall: 43, 58, 71, 85, 93, 106, 110, 120
North Wind Pictures Archive: 26
Trip Photographic Agency: 1, 4, 7, 10, 11, 12, 24, 29, 46, 51, 52, 70, 81, 102, 113, 115

ACKNOWLEDGMENTS
The author acknowledges with gratitude the many informative discussions held over two years with Sherub Wangchuck and the inspiration of Francoise Pommaret's writings.